Y0-BCO-556

ADD
JUSTICE
TO YOUR SHOPPING LIST

ADD
JUSTICE
TO YOUR SHOPPING LIST

*A guide
for reshaping
food buying habits*

Marilyn Helmuth Voran

Commissioned by the Mennonite Central Committee
Development Education Office

HERALD PRESS
Scottdale, Pennsylvania
Kitchener, Ontario

this book has been
Donated
in
Loving
Memory
of

Candace Lyn Johnson

Contents

Author's Preface

In the beginning God said, "I have provided all kinds of grain and all kinds of fruit for you to eat" (Genesis 1:29, paraphrased). Undoubtedly God intended that all earth's people should have access to the earth's food resources. But the earth's food resources today are increasingly being used as raw materials for amassing wealth and power for a few while large masses of people lack access to an adequate food supply. Much of the ongoing hunger in our world is caused not by a failure of nature, but a failure of human nature.

This booklet examines our North American food production and distribution system in relation to how it has been affected by a crisis of values in our society. We live in a society in which economic activity, irrespective of purpose, is central. This is what philosopher-writer-priest John Kavanaugh calls the "commodity form,"[1] a way of life in which the preeminent values are marketability and consumption. People are not valued as unique and irreplaceable beings, but as objects whose value depends on how much they market, produce, and consume. I believe that Christians are called to resist conforming to such a false value scheme wherever it tries to work itself into our lives, and especially where it connects with the very sustenance on which our lives depend—our food.

Media advertising would lull us into believing that the food industry "does it all for us." For a more realistic statement we should browse through a food industry trade magazine such as *Food Technology,* noticing the emphasis on increasing profit by reducing quality without the consumer noticing. Here's one example:

> Stretch your powder dollar.... C & K's new Cheddar Cheese powder enhancer can reduce up to 40% of the cheese powder formulated in a variety of food applications.... The cheddar cheese enhancer extends the flavor effectiveness while providing a significant cost savings to the food processor without loss in quality.[2]

From the consumer's point of view a 40 percent reduction in the amount of cheese in a product is a significant nutritional loss and therefore a loss in quality. But in this instance the food industry admits no connection between nutritional value and product quality.

The same attitude shows on page after page throughout the magazine.

> Magnify flavor impact.... Magnasweet flavor enhancers work by softening harsh flavors and masking unpleasant tastes of artificial sweeteners ... or synthetic flavors. Magnasweets often allow you to reduce the amount of expensive ingredients [real food] you use.[3]

> How to make "Chicken Soup" without the "middle-man." Turn ordinary noodle soup into "chicken" noodle soup— egg drop soup into "chicken" egg drop soup.... Cysteine from Nepra can enhance meat and poultry flavors of gravies, soups, processed meats, and pet foods.[4]

It is hard to find a direct link between much of what the food industry produces and what people really need. There does exist, however, a direct link between our food system and hungry people in Third World countries which Christians need to understand and respond to thoughtfully. We need to listen to the leaders of native people crying out against "progress" in the form of

> large single-crop agribusiness concerns that use up huge tracts of native lands for the growing of export crops . . . to sell to the population of industrialized societies, while the lands of the native peoples are continually reduced, their populations are crowded into ever-diminishing parcels of land, and they are then blamed for causing their own misery through overpopulation.[5]

I hope this booklet will encourage us as Christians to regard our food purchases as votes for a set of values and to add "do justice" to our shopping lists.

The writing of this booklet was commissioned by the Mennonite Central Committee (MCC), Akron, Pennsylvania. The vision for a consumer shopping guide which would go beyond the usual considerations of economy and nutrition in food buying came from the MCC's Development Education Office. Much of the resource material used in writing as well as ongoing encouragement and guidance were supplied to me by Jocele and Art Meyer, codirectors of the Development Education Office during the time the book was being written. I am grateful for the opportunity of working with MCC and the Meyers on this assignment.

Marilyn Voran
Goshen, Indiana

ADD
JUSTICE
TO YOUR SHOPPING LIST

1.

Shop for Economy, Nutrition . . . And Justice?

If you are like most North American consumers you plan your weekly supermarket excursions with care. You keep a shopping list of supplies that need replenishing. You plan meals that feature foods on "special" each week. You buy quantities of food bargains that can be frozen or stored for later use, while at the same time balancing family likes and dislikes with nutritional needs. It can take considerable time and energy to make your food dollars provide family pleasing, nutritionally sound meals in the face of constantly rising food prices.

Having met this challenge you can feel well satisfied with your shopping skills—or can you? Do you take time to consider that the simple act of grocery shopping puts you in touch with environmental and social justice issues not only in your own country but also in distant parts of the world? Are you conscious that as you travel a few hundred feet up and down the supermarket aisles you are connecting with land and people thousands of miles away?

It was not always this way. There was a time when most of what people ate grew within view of their kitchen windows or was purchased at stores stocked with regional produce. Only foods that could not be grown locally were imported from distant states or countries. Most North Americans have paid little attention to the radical changes that have taken place in our food system over the last several decades. Of course we are aware that we have food variety, convenience, and abundance unknown to our grandparents. And we take for granted that food choices are no longer limited by season or geography as they once were. But we have not been aware that with each passing year control of our food production passes into fewer and fewer hands.

From Agriculture to Agribusiness

In 1945 a committee of the Agriculture Department Chamber of Commerce reported that small farm units were "economic and social liabilities." The committee, which included representatives of big business (Armour, Carnation, and Ralston Purina) recommended that between one-half and two-thirds of all farms be eliminated. Small farms did not fit well with the U.S. government's commitment to an ever expanding American economy. People who preferred farm life to any other were not considered to be good consumers.

> Often there has been developed little desire for the variety of material things associated with a higher standard of liv-

ing, if their attainment must be at the cost of that freedom which comes from self-employment and a leisurely mode of life. Very often the ambition, the energy and the managerial ability, as well as the capital and experience necessary for larger-scale production are lacking.[1]

Since World War II millions of farm families have left the land, discouraged by government farm policies which made survival difficult for small farm units. In 1935 U.S. farms numbered 6.8 million. Today there are only 2.3 million and if current trends continue one percent of a total 1.7 million farms will account for a majority of production by the year 2000.[2] Small farms are often consolidated into large-scale production units—good markets for products such as pesticides, fertilizer, large machinery, and fuel that large agribusiness corporations need to sell.

The shift from agriculture to agribusiness correlates with increasing control of all segments of the food industry by a few giant food processing companies with worldwide operations. These multinational corporations are in business not to produce food, but to produce money, using food as a vehicle for making it. No one should object to producing food for people at a profit, but when maximizing profit becomes the overriding goal, the needs of people are often disregarded.

Our Food System Contributes to World Hunger

In *Food First,* a well-documented study of the causes of world hunger, Frances Moore Lappe and Joseph Collins show that the forces shaping our food system into one of the most tightly controlled parts of our economy are the same forces that promote world hunger. These forces directly relate to hungry Haitian peasants farming unproductive hillsides, while the more fertile valleys grow crops for North American supermarkets. These forces relate directly to Philippine families living in a crowded heap of shanties in Manila—families who formerly lived simply, but with dignity. Families have been removed from their land and their houses bulldozed to make way for export crops to feed North Americans.

And here at home these same forces have imposed upon us increased and unnecessary processing, exposure to chemicals of questionable safety, less nutrition, and continually rising prices.

"By fighting the forces tightening their hold over our food economy, we are directly fighting some of the very forces that promote hunger in other countries," say Lappe and Collins.[3]

Contemplating our connections with hungry people, we find that grocery shopping takes on meaning beyond the art of skillful buying. It is not enough to shop with nutrition and economy in mind. We need to ask who benefits and who gets hurt in relation to our food purchases. Will you consider adding "do justice" to your shopping list?

"Justice"—a word frequently mentioned these days— what does it mean in relation to grocery shopping? To do justice means simply to do right, to treat fairly. Are the people who produce food for our supermarkets treated fairly? Are they granted basic human rights of access to adequate food and shelter? Do they receive a fair wage for their work, sufficient for their needs? Are the earth's resources used efficiently in our food production and distribution system? Or are they consumed recklessly as if inexhaustible?

The following chapter presents an armchair tour of a typical North American supermarket. The products on its shelves have stories to tell that help us understand the structure of our food system—who controls our food production and what the effects are on people and on the earth. We need to understand our involvement both as participants in, and victims of, a food system that has been called the most destructive as well as the most productive the world has ever known. Only through increased awareness will we begin to find ways to work for positive change in our food system.

2.

A Supermarket Tour

Years ago Native Americans foraging for food made their way along forest paths gathering the fruits of trees and bushes and searching for productive hunting areas and fishing sites. Today we gather our food in the security of the modern supermarket, following a path carefully planned by supermarket designers to insure that we arrive at the checkout counter with many more items than we had intended to buy. What impulse traps can we avoid as we make our way along the supermarket paths?

Visualize the standard supermarket layout. Around the perimeter we find fresh groceries: baked goods, meat, eggs, dairy products, fruits, and vegetables. In the middle of the store nonperishable products in boxes, cans, and cartons fill the shelves of long, unbroken aisles. Now imagine this design reversed. The shelves of nonperishables are around the store's perimeter, with islands of dairy products, baked goods, and produce located in the center of the store. According to a USDA Economic Research Center study, the latter design would cut the typical shopper's grocery bill by one third. The study, conducted by following shoppers around the redesigned supermarket in several states, showed that the amount of money spent is determined by the distance shoppers travel—not by how long they linger in the store.

Of the thousands of items on supermarket shelves, several dozen might qualify as necessities. The standard supermarket design leads shoppers through long lanes of unneeded, but tempting, products in order to check off even a short shopping list. The USDA experimental design broke up the long trek through the store with central fresh food displays (products which people need to purchase most frequently). As a result the average purchase fell from 18 different items to 14 in the same amount of time and the checkout total dropped 33 percent. In addition to basic layout, the supermarket effectively employs a variety of other techniques to insure a higher check-out total than we had intended.

Shopping carts near the entrance filled with canned goods, cookies or crackers, soup or soap, suggest reduced prices and encourage you to stock up on items you were not planning to buy. End of aisle displays of high profit margin items also are used to suggest reduced prices which may or may not be true.

Staple items (flour, salt, etc.) are displayed on low or high shelves while luxury cake and frosting mixes are de-liberately placed at eye level.

Expensive gourmet salad dressings are displayed in the produce section next to the lettuce and tomatoes.

Quantity prices suggest savings but look carefully—do you really want two for 39¢ instead of one for 19¢?

Super, giant economy size cans or cartons sometimes cost more per ounce than smaller sizes.

Magazines and newspapers screaming sensational headlines, candy bars and other nonnutritious snacks, breath fresheners and dehydrated meatsticks tempt you as well as restless children while standing in the checkout line. Whether considered manipulation or sound business practice, strategies which promote impulse buying are not in the best interests of the consumer. Consumer research shows that from 50 to 70 percent of all supermarket purchases are of an impulse nature. Perhaps we should learn to think of the supermarket as a hostile environment. Your best protection is a thoughtfully prepared shopping list to guide you safely around the supermarket traps.

Fresh Produce Department

Imports: Whom Do They Help? Upon entering the store chosen for our armchair tour we are directed first through the house plant and flower area, a high profit margin, impulse buying section. The usual markup on plants is 35-40 percent compared with about 17 percent average markup on food.

Chrysanthemums, carnations, roses—where have all the flowers come from? Although these are the kinds of flowers most widely grown by U.S. growers, it is quite likely that this large supermarket chain retails flowers grown in Latin American countries.

In Colombia, the largest supplier of flowers to the U.S. market, 70 percent of the agricultural land is controlled by a few wealthy landowners who do not experience the struggle for food most Colombians know. By growing carnations for export, they reap 80 percent more profit per acre than by growing corn or wheat. Thus less and less land is available for growing food for hungry Colombians.

Large U.S. agribusiness companies such as Sears and Pillsbury, see the profitability of retailing these imported flowers in supermarket chains and franchised flower shops. U.S. flower growers, unable to compete with inexpensive imports, which reflect low labor costs, are forced out of business.

Suggestions for Responsible Shopping

1. **Find out where your supermarket's flowers are grown.**

2. **Buy U.S.-grown flowers. They will be more expensive but let's face it—fresh flowers out of season are a luxury on which we should expect a luxury price tag. When we are offered bargain prices on luxury items we need to question whether someone is getting the bad end of the bargain.**

Fruits and Vegetables. As attractive as the flower display is the selection of fresh fruits and vegetables adjoining it. Asparagus, broccoli, cauliflower, cucumbers, eggplant, several varieties of leaf and head lettuce, and on through the alphabet to strawberries, tomatoes and zucchini, with most of them available the year around. Until recent years we could assume that winter vegetables came from the Sunbelt states, but that is no longer true as large growers have shifted operations to low-cost, "offshore" production sites in Latin American countries. Mexico, for example, grows half of the winter tomatoes sold in the U.S. and a third of our annual strawberry and cantaloupe consumption is supplied by Mexican land and labor. Onion, cucumber, eggplant, and squash imports from Latin American countries have increased 10-43 percent depending on which vegetable you are looking at.

Growing crops for North American supermarkets is negatively affecting the availability of basic foods for native people. In Mexico in the 1970s, the rate of deaths from malnutrition in early childhood increased 70 percent while acreages of wheat, corn, beans, and rice declined 25 percent. The change in production priorities has made the cost of even the lowly rice and bean diet a luxury that many of the poor cannot afford. It is an added irony that 65 percent of the fruits and vegetables raised in Latin American countries are dumped or used for animal feed because of an oversupplied U.S. market or because they do not meet the beauty standards of American consumers.[1]

What is it like to work in the Mexican strawberry industry? Lappe and Collins give this glimpse into the experiences of native workers. Since the strawberry industry has come to the Zamora valley, small towns have become large towns with over three fourths of the population living in carton shack slums that ring the towns.

> No sanitation, no running water and little electricity. All in all a classic case of "over-population." Yet in Zamora you can also find the ranch style houses of the new strawberry millionaires. As employers these few individuals and their American partners directly benefit from the desperate misery of the majority.... Since the number seeking work far exceeds the number of jobs the growers are able to hold down wages. Some growers, despite the large number of unemployed in Zamora, send recruiter trucks to outlying villages because the peasants there are willing to work for still less.[2]

A golden mountain of bananas, the most important fresh fruit in world trade, calls attention to a commonly accepted myth related to export cropping. North Americans naively assume that certain developing countries are especially suited for growing one kind of crop, and therefore growing that crop for export is good for those countries' development and provides needed employment for native people. That these assumptions are quite far from the truth is clearly demonstrated in the "banana republics." What is called "prime banana land" by the banana growing companies is in fact, prime agricultural land well suited to growing a wide variety of crops needed for human nutrition. Bananas were not grown in the "banana republics" until the late 1830s when they were introduced by colonizers to whom banana trees looked like money trees.

The benefits of growing bananas for export are reaped mostly by the "big three" importing companies: United Brands (Chiquita), Castle & Cooke (Dole), and Del Monte. Only 11¢ of each dollar we pay for bananas stays in the producer country. Large multinational corporations like United Brands, Castle & Cooke, and Del Monte often have more power to control the terms of production and exporting of crops than do the governments of the countries in which they operate. This is why the Union of Banana Producing Countries were losers in the 1974 "banana war." When they tried to realize a higher return on their banana exports by asking a 50¢ per box increase in export tax, the "big 3" fought back by allowing tons of bananas to rot on the docks and bribing officials to lower the tax.

The cost of manufactured goods and foods the banana producing countries need to import is rising faster than their income from bananas. In 1960 three tons of bananas would buy a tractor, but in 1970 it took 11 tons.

Export cropping of bananas does not necessarily create jobs for native people. One reason for growing bananas is that they do not require frequent planting, thus minimizing the producers' dependence on labor. In addition to the initial low labor input, increasing mechanization has further reduced the need for labor. Today the number of laborers needed for one acre of bananas is only one fourth of what it was 40 years ago. In the summer of 1983 three thousand banana plantation workers found themselves without jobs when United Brands "peeled out of Costa Rica."[3] In a program of converting its Costa Rican holdings to African palm production which requires one third the labor of banana production, United Brands violated an agreement with the Costa Rican government to use a certain percentage of its land to grow bananas through the year 2000. The displaced workers responded with a peaceful occupation of company lands and demanded that the government expropriate United Brand's holdings and give them parcels of land to farm, but they met with little success.

Travel Worn U.S.-Grown Produce. Fruits and vegetables that are grown in the U.S. travel thousands of miles at an annual cost of 500 million gallons of expensive fuel to reach our supermarket produce departments, but much of this travel is unnecessary. For example, in a recent year New York area consumers bought about 24,000 tons of broccoli—most of it shipped 2,700 miles from California in spite of the fact that New York state has an ideal climate for growing broccoli. (In fact broccoli would grow well almost anyplace in the U.S. except southern Florida.) A trucker reports loading potatoes in Idaho for delivery in the Midwest then driving 200 miles and loading potatoes to deliver in Idaho. Northern Indiana, where apple orchards abound, offers consumers apples fresh from Washington state.

In our crazy-quilt system of food growing and distribution, for every two dollars invested in growing food we spend one dollar to move it around.[4] Such an unplanned food distribution system leaves large areas, especially cities, of our nation highly vulnerable to severe food shortages in case of natural disaster, fuel shortages, or transportation strikes.

In addition to wasting fuel resources, long-distance transportation of produce contributes to deterioration of its nutritional value. It takes five to seven days, sometimes even two weeks for fresh produce to move cross-country from field to supermarket, yet broccoli loses 19 percent of its vitamin C in just 24 hours in a refrigerator truck. Four days of travel results in a 34 percent loss of vitamin C. Asparagus in cold storage loses 19 percent of its vitamin C as well as significant amounts of vitamins A and B_1 in one week of refrigeration. Spinach after a week in cold storage is minus 29 percent of its vitamin C.[5]

Suggestions for Responsible Shopping

1. **Reduce use of Third World export crops (or stop using them altogether)—not to diminish guilt but to be consistent with your beliefs.**

2. **Pay a self-imposed "import tax" on any Third World export crops you buy—a symbolic act which can explain the causes of world hunger to children. Give the "revenue" you collect to a church or community agency serving poor people (in addition to your regular giving, of course.).**

3. **Reduce use of out-of-season produce. Plan your meals to harmonize with seasonal availabilities in your area. Delightful recipes and creative ideas for serving seasonal food are often found in the**

food columns of local newspapers. Celebrate the cycle of seasons in your meals.

4. Encourage local stores to stock locally grown produce when possible.

Bakery Department

Common sense would suggest that the baked goods be displayed near the end of your shopping path so you could place soft bakery products on top of the heavier cans and boxes in your cart. No doubt it is dollars and cents which dictates its location early on in our tour. Tempting sweet rolls, donuts, danish pastries, and "homemade" looking cookies help create a climate for impulse buying early in your shopping trip.

Our Daily Bread: Staff of Life or Fractured Food? Baking companies have responded to increasingly nutrition conscious consumers with numerous variations on the standard white loaf which give the illusion of improved nutrition, but most of which are still made largely of refined white flour. "Wheat & Honey," "Honey-bran," "Whole Meal," "Stone-ground" and other image building words appear on loaves in wrappers picturing nostalgic scenes of old mills and sheaves of wheat. There is no way to tell by looking at a loaf whether it is made largely of whole wheat flour or just colored with caramel to make you think so. The words "wheat bread" and "wheat flour" frequently used to imply whole grain nutrition are misleading. All bread is wheat bread (unless of course, it is made from corn or rye flour). There is still a general lack of appreciation among some consumers as well as in the baking industry for the whole wheat berry as a beautifully balanced package of important nutrients.

The largest part of a wheat berry (or other whole grain) is the white *endosperm* which becomes white flour. It is rich in starch and a protein called gluten. The nutrients found in the tiny *germ* of the wheat—iron, niacin, thiamin, and zinc—are all needed by the body before it can utilize the starch to produce energy. Also in the germ is the amino acid lysine, without which the gluten protein is severely imbalanced. But all are lost in the refinement process. Also lost in refining is the *bran* covering, an excellent source of fiber which is now being recognized for its important role in maintaining health.

When we buy bread and other products made largely of white flour we are obviously not getting full benefit of the balance of nutrients designed into the grain by a wise Creator. "Enrichment" of white flour, while returning some of the nutrients lost in refinement does not restore the nutritional balance of whole grain. If you want to buy whole grain nutrition with your food dollar look for "100% whole wheat" on the wrapper or "whole wheat flour" listed first in the ingredient statement.

The Farmer's Share. The average price of a one pound loaf of white bread increased from 27.7¢ in 1973 to 54.2¢ in 1983 according to Agriculture Department figures. But the farm value of the wheat and other farm-originated ingredients has not increased proportionately. In 1973 the farmer's share of the cost of a loaf of bread was 3.4¢ and by 1983 it has risen to 5.1¢ revealing a current farm-retail spread of 49.1¢ compared with 24.3¢ ten years ago.

Processed Foods Section

In the center section of the supermarket, long aisles of processed food in cans, cartons, and jars remind us that the fastest growing segment of the food industry produces the most intensely processed foods. As our food system moves steadily toward more highly processed foods it is becoming increasingly energy consumptive. In using 30 percent of the energy invested in the U.S. food system, processors go through countless expensive and wasteful motions of breaking down traditional foods into their components then recombining them, taking substances out, then putting them back again, or making entirely new chemical creations.

For example, in a recent issue of *Food Technology* magazine General Foods announced the perfection of a process "for preparing an enzyme saccharified ready-to-eat cereal by milling and separating a whole grain cereal to produce germ and bran and endosperm fractions for separate treatment and recombination to form a cereal dough."[6] We have a right to ask how, if at all, will this latest development in fiddling with grain benefit the consumer. And how will it affect the nutritional composition of the grain—or the price of a box of Post's cereal?

Looking over the shelves of processed foods we can easily sense what are the advantages of highly processed foods to the manufacturer. Processed foods lend themselves readily to assembly line production and mass marketing techniques. Pringles can be manufactured by the billions, all identical, stacking themselves compactly into tennis ball cans which can be conveniently stockpiled and shipped as needed to supermarkets all over the U.S. Processed foods can stay on shelves an incredibly long time thanks to the success of food technology in inventing methods to keep foods "fresh" for two or more years. When was the last time you bought a box of cereal with the intention of keeping it for even six months?

Paying for the Package. Packaging for a proliferation of

processed foods not only consumes additional large amounts of energy and other resources, but it also adds to our country's already staggering solid waste disposal burden and adds significantly to food prices. It doesn't matter to the food processor that packaging can cost more than the ingredients inside. The cost is easily passed on to consumers. And packaging sells the product. Would anyone buy at $2.87 a pound a plain package of noodles with a few pinches of dehydrated sauce and seasoning mix? But those ingredients in a box bearing a full-color picture of a steaming tasty looking dish sell very well as "Hamburger Helper."

Watch out for this "new concept" in packaging offered to the food companies by the Packaging Corporation of America:

> Cans may be packaged in cardboard cartons to improve product display. The carton's four flat panels show pictures of the product better than can be done on a rounded can. Although the cartoned can occupies the same shelf space as the can alone, it looks larger and more impressive. A perforated tear tape at the top of the carton facilitates easy removal for consumer convenience.[7]

Consumers will pay for this excess packaging which persuaded them to buy the product, and will no doubt appreciate the "convenience" of ripping off the tear tape before applying a can opener to the can.

One dollar out of every eleven spent by consumers on groceries goes for packaging, most of which is thrown away. This figures out to $400 per year for a family of four. When you buy soft drinks or gelatin dessert and pudding mixes you pay twice as much for the package as for the contents. Ready-to-eat-cereals and baby foods come in packaging costing one and one-half times as much as their contents. On the other hand, the ratio of packaging costs to contents for meat, fresh produce, cheese, flour, sugar, and other basic commodities is only from 3 to 7 percent.

Suggestions for Responsible Shopping

1. **Avoid buying products which come in packages that cost more than their contents.**

2. **Avoid overpackaged foods—cans in cardboard cartons, individually wrapped cheese slices, foil wrapped cream cheese in cardboard carton, etc.**

3. **When there is a choice buy products in glass instead of plastic. Glass can be recycled. Plastic is made from nonrenewable resources and can not be recycled.**

The Food Giants: Survival of the Biggest. Noticing many different brand names on boxes, cartons, and cans we might get the impression of thousands of companies in keen competition. It is a false impression. Of 30,000 food processing companies in the U.S. a mere one percent of them own practically every nationwide brand and 50 national processors earn 90 percent of the industry profits. An industry group is considered capable of monopolistic pricing when four firms control 35 percent of the market. In almost every food line four firms control 55 percent or more of the market. Government statistics indicate that American consumers are overcharged 14-16 million dollars annually (about $313 for a family of four) because of concentration in the food industry.

With each passing year control of our food is concentrated into fewer and fewer hands. This is not surprising. In a society organized as ours is, on the basis of unlimited growth and competition for accumulation of profit, the strategy for survival and prosperity in the food industry must include getting control of more and more of the market.

A highly successful strategy for gaining market power is merger. Larger companies buy up smaller ones, creating huge consumer product conglomerates which monopolize the supermarket shelves with thousands of brands of highly advertised products. You could do your entire grocery shopping and end up buying the products of only a few powerful companies.

The two largest conglomerates are European based. Unilever, a British-Dutch corporation, owns such brands as Lipton tea and soups, Imperial margarine, Lucky Whip topping, Mrs. Butterworth's syrup, Wish-Bone salad dressings, Knox gelatin, to name only a few. There are only eight countries in the world whose annual GNP is larger than Unilever's assets.[8] The Nestle company is a Swiss corporation holding Nestea, Libby, McNeil & Libby, Stouffer frozen foods and restaurants, and Taster's Choice coffee along with other well-known brands.

The largest U.S. conglomerate bears a name few people ever heard of before the Beatrice TV ad campaign projecting an image of a benevolent corporation supplying consumers with a wide range of products essential for living the "good life." Beginning as a small butter and egg farm in Beatrice, Nebraska, Beatrice picked up products such as LaChoy Chinese foods, Canada Dry and Schweppes, Dannon Yogurt, RC Cola, Sunbeam Bread, Clark Bars, Aunt Nellie's vegetables, Martha White flour, Airstream Trailers, Samsonite luggage, and Eckrich meats to name just a few of its over 400 "profit centers." But that was not enough. Beatrice recently purchased the Esmark Corporation, another conglomerate whose holdings include such consumer products as Peter Pan Peanut Butter, Orville Redenbacher popping corn, Playtex intimate apparel, Danskin knitwear, Max Factor cosmetics, and Swift-Hunt-Wesson. By adding Swift's strong meat business to its own Eckrich, Beatrice will greatly increase its share of the meat market.

Hundreds of millions of dollars are invested in company takeovers—not to build new factories, nor to create new jobs for unemployed workers, but to change names on some deeds and to buy instant market expansion and cash flow for the giant conglomerate. For 152 million dollars Pillsbury bought control of Green Giant, instantly gaining a nationwide processed vegetable market. The R. J. Reynolds tobacco company branched out into food by coming up with 621 million dollars to take control of Del Monte, the world's most powerful producer of processed fruits and vegetables. The rising prices we pay at the checkout counter help finance companies' takeover campaigns.

A second cost to consumers rises out of the future market power conglomerates gain through merger. Beatrice, for example, with its hundreds of "profit centers" can collect and reshuffle profits, distributing them where they will do the most good. "It is likely," quips investigative journalist Daniel Zwerdling, "that the rising price you pay for Dannon Yogurt has less to do with the state of the nation's udders than with the cash flow needs of Samsonite luggage."[9] And in the same vein, he asks, "How much of the premium price you paid for Minute Maid orange juice—it costs 30 percent more than the store brand at my local Safeway—was dictated by the sun and bugs on Coca-Cola's orange groves in Florida? And how much was ... tacked on to finance 'free' soccer games and clinics for children in Africa and the Middle East to build the Coca-Cola name abroad?"[10]

Advertising: Serving Consumers or the Corporation? Many consumers recognize that there is something insincere—even ridiculous—about processed food ads, but are not aware of the vital role they play in corporate control of our food and in the steady rise in food prices. The annual cost of food advertising is 7-9 billion dollars. About 8 percent of that is used to advertise fresh and relatively unprocessed food. The rest goes to promote heavily processed food products. When you buy heavily advertised, highly processed foods, the cost to you for advertising that persuaded you to buy the products will be from 6 to 35 cents of every dollar spent.

If food advertising offered useful product information it might be worth paying for, but it is hard to find food ads that serve us in that way. There is virtually no nutrition information and (except for newspapers) little price information in food advertising. It is mainly image building and its overall informational value is usually marginal. A TV ad for Minute Rice, a compelling rhythmic chant—"Minute Rice fits the way you want to cook today"—repeated about a half dozen or more times during the ad, does not help you evaluate whether its $1.36 a pound price tag is a good food buy when you can buy regular rice for under 40¢ a pound. An ad presenting Cool Whip as the key ingredient in elegant desserts links Cool Whip with creativity—"a little of us and a little of you"—but does not help you judge whether its long list of chemical ingredients represents a better food investment than plain whipping cream which you can whip in five minutes.

But advertising does serve the giant food corporations very well. They have learned that they can win control of a targeted market if only they spend enough for advertising and promotion. The coffee display calls our attention to how consumers and small independent companies fare when caught in the crossfire of large companies' advertising wars. As recently as 15 years ago about 100 companies shared in the coffee market. Now there are less than 40 companies roasting and selling coffee in the U.S.

Some of the casualties fell in the Proctor & Gamble-General Foods coffee war of the 1970s. It all began when P & G, already the holder of leading brands used from kitchen to bathroom in American homes, coveted the coffee market. It didn't matter that P & G didn't own an ounce of coffee or that General Foods (Maxwell House) was already the nation's most powerful coffee marketer. P & G knew well the power of its conglomerate advertising budget. After buying out J. A. Folger, a family-owned southwest regional coffee company, P & G began promoting the Folger brand with one of the most intensive ad and promotional campaigns the food industry has ever known. In its ad blitz against General Foods, P & G saturated industrial cities of the East with Mrs. Olsen on TV, with free samples mailed to homes, and with discount coupons and special deals. General Foods of course retaliated with similar tactics, crushing local companies in the way.

In 1977 P & G reportedly lost 60 million dollars on the Folger subsidiary because it spent so much buying ads and slashing prices. But it did not really lose the money. Consumers financed the coffee war by paying inflated prices for Duncan Hines cake mixes and other leading P & G products. The conglomerate merely shifted its profits where they were needed to carry on the coffee war.

More Imports. The coffee display and also the nearby tea and cocoa shelves remind us again of our connections with hungry people in the Caribbean area, in Central and South American countries, and in Africa where these kitchen staples are grown for us at the expense of food crops for local use. We note too that while processing of cocoa beans into products such as cocoa powder, baking chocolate, and candy bars is a highly profitable industry, most cocoa producing countries are effectively cut out of these profits because of restrictive tariff laws. For example, U.S. tariffs on candy bars are five times higher than on cocoa beans. The cocoa producing countries end up selling most of their cocoa production as raw beans to processors such as Hershey and Nestles and Cadbury who then realize large profits from cocoa products they make.

Coupons: Who Wins, Who Loses? Many products in the processed foods section of the supermarket can be purchased at reduced prices with cents-off coupons clipped from magazines and newspapers. Coupons give the consumer the feeling of having saved money and give the food company a benevolent image with the consumer, but coupons should be regarded as advertising—a promotional technique benefiting the manufacturer more than consumers. Before you spend time clipping coupons compare brand-name products offering cents-off coupons with similar generic or house brands. You will find that in many cases the brand-name product costs more even with the coupon.

Coupons, instead of cutting your grocery bill, can actually increase it if you buy products you would not ordinarily buy just because you have a coupon.

Although individual consumers may benefit from coupons if they use them judiciously, consumers as a class pay for the savings realized by coupon users because the price consumers pay for food must include all costs including the cost of coupons. Coupons do not generally reach the poor who can hardly afford the necessities, let alone magazines and newspapers, the major sources of coupons. Coupon redemption rates are three to four times higher in higher income areas. Those who do not use coupons, often the poor, subsidize the savings of the coupon user.

Coupons are not gifts from a benevolent industry, but part of a company's strategy to gain more control of a targeted market. Recently a coupon worth 50¢ toward Proctor & Gamble's new Citrus Hill Orange Juice arrived in the mail. I have mixed feelings about redeeming it. Although it represents a significant saving on a basic food (especially if redeemed at the store offering double coupon savings this weekend), I am reluctant to cooperate with P & G in its campaign to capture a large share of the orange juice market with this promotional strategy.

Suggestions for Responsible Shopping

1. **When there is a choice between highly advertised brands and generic or house brands of equal quality, buy generic.**

2. **Talk back to food ads. Identify the fake needs created and the false promises made.**

3. **Distinguish between the actual contents of a package and the image being sold by the pictures on the packaging.**

4. **Before using coupons for brand name products, compare the prices of generic or house brands.**

5. **If you know someone who needs coupon savings more than you do, give them your coupons.**

Product Differentiation: New, Improved, Better Than Ever? To make their advertising dollars pay off, the food companies must persuade consumers that they are selling something new. "Product differentiation" is the industry term. The way to differentiate basic foods is to process them, giving them a new shape, texture, taste, or greater convenience. Food marketers spend millions of dollars to discover those needs and desires of consumers ready to be tapped by the latest processed food novelty. At Standard Brands the research staff has increased 60 percent in the past few years. General Foods spends 70 million dollars a year in new product research. These costs are of course added to the price we pay for food.

During World War II the food industry developed necessary technology to process foods for easy shipping, safe storage, and convenient preparation in order to feed U.S. servicemen at home and overseas. When the war ended the industry could turn its attention to the wide open market of consumers at home, waiting to be sold "convenience." But often what we are offered is just an illusion of convenience. Many convenience foods simply allow you to trade cutting and peeling time for shopping and lugging time. Hamburger Helper is a classic example of a convenience food that isn't all that convenient. You still have to supply the meat and brown it and cook the noodles. Almost anyone can learn how to add seasonings (minus unnecessary chemicals) that flavor the varieties of Hamburger Helper and its relative, Tuna Helper.

Many convenience products are fabricated, and imitation foods of low nutritional quality are "fortified" to give the illusion of nutrition. Take Tang for example. An orange has a variety of nutrients, but Tang is not an orange. No matter how much vitamin C and A it is fortified with it cannot be made into an orange. If we substitute Tang for oranges we lose important nutrients from our diet that some other food will have to make up. Pop Tarts and Breakfast Squares are essentially candy breakfasts concocted from sugar and saturated fats. Although "fortified" with some vitamins and minerals, they do not come close to offering the nutritional balance of the simplest whole grain toast or muffin breakfast.

Do you ever wonder what changes occur in the nutritional composition of food subjected to the ever increasing onslaughts of processing? What happens to the essential vitamins, the protein forming amino acids, and body regulating trace minerals in a kernel of corn or wheat subjected to temperatures as high as 500° and pressure up to 40 tons in the rolling, crushing, shredding, and toasting processes they go through to become transformed into ready to eat cereal? Acknowledging reason for concern, the FDA announced early in 1984 a plan to "conduct research on effects of manufacturing, processing, and preservation on nutrients and other food components of public health interest."[11]

Fabricated, imitation, super-processed foods go hand in hand with increasing corporate control of our food system. Corporate plans for unlimited growth and greater market control call for an increasing emphasis on highly processed foods. This was one of the findings of the 1978 U.S. Senate Committee on Nutrition and Human Need which was not included in the published report. In a preliminary study commissioned by the committee, economist John Connor wrote, "The strong association of poor nutritional quality with both high and increasing [corporate] concentration remains irrefutable. If present trends continue [toward increasing concentration] the nation can expect a worsening situation."[12]

Suggestions for Responsible Shopping

1. Instead of buying convenience foods try "batch cooking." Cook multiple quantities of soup and casserole recipes on days when you do have time to cook. Freeze them in meal-size portions for later convenience. Obviously this strategy requires planning ahead to have on hand the necessary ingredients in quantities needed.

2. Invest time in making your own nutritious convenience mixes—free from unnecessary additives. (See recipe section.)

3. Shape your own cookie dough into rolls and freeze for quick slicing and baking when cookies are needed on the spur of the moment.

4. Ignore tempting recipes printed in newspaper and magazine food pages that call for highly processed convenience foods such as ready-to-eat cereals, "tater tots," whipped topping mix, pudding mix, canned soup, etc., as main ingredients. When you want to add interest to meals with new recipes, turn to collections such as *More-with-Less Cookbook* which emphasize the use of relatively unprocessed cooking ingredients.

Ready-to-Eat Cereals. The breakfast cereal section displays more than 130 different varieties and sizes of cereal. On the middle shelves at children's eye-level are expensive sugared cereals. Four firms (General Mills, Post, Kelloggs, and Quaker Oats) control almost 86 percent of the cereal market. Here we have one of the most glaring examples of monopolistic practices in the food industry. The FTC has charged that the four firms have acted as though they were a single company monopolizing the industry, earning above normal profits, excluding new competitors, and overcharging consumers. The overcharge, estimated at one million dollars a year, results from prices set higher than they would be if the industry were competitive.

Price competition cannot exist in the cereal industry because it would not benefit anyone (except the consumer). If General Mills wanted to increase its share of the cereal market, it could lower its prices to attract new buyers, but since the other three would immediately lower theirs the outcome would be that each company would still have the same share of the market, but with less profit. So a company competes by flooding the market with "new products." As a strategy statement from Kellogg's ad agency in the late 1960s put it, "Continued proliferation of the presweet business [children's presweetened cereals] through consecutive new product introduction is the essence of competitive strategy."[13]

But how many "new products" can a company make from a few basic grains? The possibilities seem endless. Remember Kix, a plain puffed corn cereal? General Mills added an artificial fruit flavor and called it Trix. The same cereal with chocolate flavor was Cocoa Puffs. Kix sprayed with vitamins and minerals becomes Body Buddies which were further differentiated into Body Buddies with brown sugar and honey and Body Buddies with natural fruit flavor.

The growing "market segment" which wants a high fiber cereal has inspired an amazing differentiation of bran cereal. No longer is the choice simply 40 percent or 100 percent bran. There is a bran for those who want it sweetened with honey and for those who prefer it sweetened with fig and prune juice. Those who are particular about shape can have it as buds, flakes, or chex. And those who have grown bored with the flavor of wheat bran can now switch to corn bran. The big four companies are locked into a never-ending spiral of new product development with their accompanying high marketing costs which are passed on to the consumer. That explains why the average price of cereal today is four times as high as in 1953, while the consumer price index for food purchased to be used at home has tripled in the same period.

Canned Fruits and Vegetables. Although there are 1,200 companies producing canned fruits and vegetables in the U.S., nine of them take 50 percent of the market. (Del Monte alone accounts for 16 percent.) Big processors like Del Monte, Campbells, General Foods, and Heinz, maximize profits by keeping the price they pay for farm goods at a minimum. Their strategy for doing this is the production contract. Three fourths of the vegetables produced in the U.S. are grown by farmers under contract to large corporations. The farmers have little opportunity to negotiate the terms of the contract. If they try to organize to ask for better prices for their product or more satisfactory terms the company is likely to hasten its move to "offshore production sites." Such was the case when Del Monte began its move to Mexico after growers in Washington and Oregon organized into a bargaining association and won a price increase.

Since its entrance into Mexico, Del Monte has consistently contracted with the largest landowners because it is much easier to supervise production on a smaller number of large farms than on a greater number of small farms. As wealthy farmers have become wealthier they have succeeded in buying land from smaller farmers to whom any cash offer looked good even though selling their land made them landless farm laborers with less food security.

In the Philippines Del Monte has exerted pressure on small subsistence farmers to coerce them to lease their fields to Philpak (Del Monte's Philippine subsidiary). In some cases guards drove cattle over the farmer's planted fields, and sprayed fields with crop-killing chemicals. Farmers eventually realized they had little choice except to lease their land and work as laborers for the company. Fr. Edward Gerlock, who has worked with many dispossessed Philippine farmers, estimates that in 1977 a farmer on one hectare could, by growing two crops a year earn about $600 annually. But when the farmer leases this hectare to the company at between 30-70 dollars and works as a laborer he can earn only about $420 a year even if he works 350 days a year. And now he has to buy food staples which he used to raise himself.[14]

The Campbells label, so prominent in the canned soup and tomato products displays, profits from its "Labels for Education" program. Through this program Campbells enjoys the services of children and school personnel promoting and creating a market for Campbells products which include foods bearing the names Franco American, Bounty, Pepperidge Farms, and Swansons. Mrs. Pauls frozen fish, Vlasic pickles, and Le Menu frozen dinners also come from Campbells. In return for many hours spent urging parents, friends, and school food service buyers to purchase Campbells products, the school may redeem labels to get a piece of educational or athletic equipment. Since consumers pay from 2 to 15¢ more for Campbells products than for other brands, the cost of the "free" equipment often totals more than if the equipment were bought through regular school purchasing channels.

The Campbells label also calls to mind the concerns of an estimated 30,000 migrant farm workers who labor in tomatoes, cucumbers, apples, and other crops grown in Midwestern states. While making a significant contribution to the nation's diet they themselves suffer from undernutrition. Poverty level income, substandard living conditions, and exposure to dangerous pesticides are part of their lives. As one of the largest tomato processors in the U.S., Campbells is the target of a farm worker strike and nationwide boycott by the Farm Labor Organizing Committee, an organization whose goals are to achieve human dignity and social justice for farm workers. Products of Libby, McNeil & Libby, owned by Nestle Company, are included in the boycott.

FLOC believes the companies should take some responsibility for the low wages and unsatisfactory working and living conditions of migrant workers in Ohio, Indiana, and southern Michigan. Although Campbells does not own the tomato fields or hire workers, it does control the terms of the contracts with growers who hire farm workers and in that way controls how much the growers can pay for labor and what kinds of benefits are offered. FLOC intends to continue the boycott and strike until Campbells agrees to enter into three-way negotiations involving farm workers and growers.

After learning about the boycott issue, 52 percent of the public schools in Indianapolis that were collecting Campbells labels dropped the program and almost all the schools in the archdiocese of Indianapolis decided not to participate in the labels program. Across the U.S. other school systems, especially religious schools, are refraining from participation in the labels program, believing that promoting Campbells products can be seen as indifference to the needs of farm workers.

Soft Drinks. At the soft drink display, consider again the people in Third World countries. Soft drink companies, primarily Coca-Cola and Pepsi, have successfully marketed (or unscrupulously pushed) their nonnutritious products in Africa, the Middle East, and Latin America. Massive ad campaigns have convinced the poor that soft drinks are a symbol of the good life. Made of inexpensive ingredients (sugar and water) they can be priced within reach of millions of poor and still return a substantial profit to the manufacturers. With saturation advertising, Coke and Pepsi dominate the market—not the local soft drink brands. Coca-Cola's advertisers note with satisfaction that a Palestinian refugee shining shoes in Beirut saves his piastres for a real Coca-Cola at twice the price of a local cola.[15]

Suggestions for Responsible Shopping

1. **Buy real fruit juices instead of soft drinks. Spend your food dollars for good nutrition—not just sugar and water.**

2. **Use more of the original thirst quencher—water.**

This ends the supermarket tour. We have tried to recognize our connections (unintentional as they are) with exploitation and injustice in Third World countries. We have also identified some ways that we ourselves are victimized by our food system. Now we face the question of how should we respond. What can we do to work toward a more just and sustainable food system?

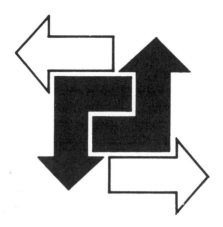

3.
Work for Change

Speaking to a conference of major Christian churches in Canada studying hunger and justice issues, economist Susan George commented that "too many people, especially church people, are dealing only with personal guilt. Corporate action aimed at deeper structural changes has to become a priority."

She further observed that "our Christian theology gives us such a sense of hope that we believe anything is possible."[1] She suggested that Christians should learn how the food system works, how to regain a measure of control, and how to help the multinationals operate in just ways abroad.

Regain a Measure of Control

A first step toward regaining some control of our food is to question how much we want to accept from the giant food companies. To what extent do we want to subsidize their multimillion dollar take-over and advertising campaigns and their wasteful proliferation of food novelties? This is an important step not because it will change the food industry, but because it will change us. When I buy oranges or orange juice instead of Tang, General Foods will not notice, but internally I feel a lot more consistent (not to mention better fed).

Frances Lappe reminds us that choosing to consume in a manner consistent with our understanding of the problems need not be to reduce personal guilt, but to diminish feelings of powerlessness. "To realize that we can make some real choices is a first step in regaining a sense of personal power in face of a system that denies individual responsibility for our choices."[2]

Shopping with justice in mind will sometimes mean choosing less convenience. Some choices might be more expensive. But let us not be disturbed by the thought of change. Remember that our eating and shopping habits have changed drastically in the last several decades. The food industry has persuaded consumers to buy more and more processed foods and fewer basic commodities. In order to continue growth the industry needs to keep us moving in that direction. The question is, who will be in charge of change—the food technologists and advertising agencies or you and I? We can consider it a blessing to be in charge of changes we choose to make.

Go on a New Diet: The Local Diet. Farm markets have almost doubled in number in most states in recent years. More consumers are regaining a measure of control of their food by direct purchasing from the farmer and eliminating costs generated by packing, brokering, wholesaling, distributing, advertising, and retailing. The farmers receive more return for their work and the consumer enjoys more satisfactory food at lower cost. "The best tasting food ripens on the vine, not in refrigerator trucks crossing the country," comments one farm-market enthusiast. A number of states publish farm market guides to put consumers in touch with farms within driving distance where they can pick quantities of fruits and vegetables for canning and freezing. Ask your county agriculture agent for information about obtaining a farm market guide for your area.

Join a Food Co-op. In the past decade thousands of food co-ops and buying clubs have grown up in cities and towns around the country. By purchasing in bulk from local sources as much as possible and doing their own packaging consumers save as much as 30 percent on basic foods. These may include fresh produce, meat, eggs, cheese, honey, grains, beans, nuts, and dried fruits. Food co-ops often stock important staples usually not available in supermarkets—for example a wide variety of whole grain flours. To bake muffins, cookies, cakes, or pastry of delicate texture without using refined white flour, you can choose finely ground whole *wheat pastry flour.* To bake yeasted breads you can use whole wheat bread flour. Because of its high gluten content it will produce loaves of pleasing texture without addition of refined white flour. In addition to significant savings in food costs, co-op members value the fellowship of friends working together to regain a measure of control over their food supply.

Information on organizing and operating a food co-op is available from the following sources:

Community Services Administration
1200 19th St. NW, Room 318 B
Washington, DC 20506
Publications: *How to Organize a Co-op,
Moving Ahead Together,* and others

Food Co-ops for Small Groups, by Tony Velella.
Workman Publishing Co.
231 East 51st St.
New York, NY 10022

Food Co-ops Handbook, NEFCO Collective
2 Park St.
Boston, MA 02101

Help Multinational Corporations Operate Fairly

The first step in helping multinationals operate in just
ways abroad is to overcome feelings of powerlessness that
most of us have. The success of the 6½-year-long boycott
of Nestle products demonstrated that concerned citizens
can exert the moral and economic pressure to convince
powerful multinationals to act more responsibly toward the
poor of developing countries. The Nestle boycott was
begun on July 4, 1977, by a small grass roots organization
called the Infant Formula Action Coalition. It called attention to the problem of bottle baby disease resulting from
the marketing of infant formula in Third World countries.
Since the 1950s health researchers had identified bottle feeding as a major cause of infant diarrhea, malnutrition, and
death. Yet even in the face of the evidence, infant formula
manufacturers continued to promote their product as better
for the baby than breast feeding, even though poor families
could hardly afford to buy formula. The boycott spread to
ten countries with one million people participating. According to *Newsweek,* Nestle spent tens of millions of dollars
resisting the boycott.[3] Finally on January 25, 1984, the boy-

cott was suspended after Nestle representatives publicly announced their willingness to implement a marketing code drawn up by the World Health Organization of UNICEF. Congratulating the boycott supporters INFACT wrote:

> What you have achieved is a remarkable unprecedented success. . . . Without the use of force, without the authority of law you . . . have helped to save the lives of millions of babies throughout the world. . . . You have reversed the balance of power in the struggle to save the victims of bottle baby disease. Now that Nestle has been convinced to implement the WHO code they have a vested interest in seeing that its competitors abide by the code as well. . . . We have turned an opponent into an ally.[4]

INFACT plans to continue working to help multinationals act more responsibly abroad. More information can be obtained from:

INFACT Clearinghouse
1701 University Ave. SE
Minneapolis, MN 55414

The boycott of Campbell's and Libby's products by the Farm Labor Organizing Committee was mentioned earlier in this booklet. More background information about the farm workers' problems and FLOC's efforts to bring about three-way negotiations involving the processing companies, the growers, and the farm workers is available from:

FLOC
714½ S. St. Clair
Toledo, OH 43609

Influence Government Policy

Bread for the World, a Christian citizens' movement, has had notable success in influencing U.S. government policies that affect hungry people. Its monthly newsletters and study papers contain reliable information about world events, especially events related to world hunger. Action pieces inform members of upcoming legislation related to these issues and encourage members to write or call their representatives in Congress.

Though the legislative process might seem bewilderingly complex it does work and Bread for the World helps it work for hungry people. Bread for the World lobbies from a position of faith, believing that Christians should use their citizenship to influence policy and that this is a way of helping others that is consistent with the gospel of Jesus. Membership in Bread for the World ($25) includes a subscription to the newsletter and study papers. Write to:

Bread for the World
802 Rhode Island Ave., NE
Washington, DC 20018

Increase Understanding

The Institute for Food and Development Policy is a nonprofit research and documentation and education center for issues that link together U.S. agriculture, hunger in America, and world hunger. It is an excellent source of well researched information that can deepen our understanding of the causes of hunger here and abroad. The Institute has recently published the *Food First Curriculum,* a valuable resource for teaching children about hunger issues, using an approach that links children's experiences with global concerns. Designed for sixth-grade students the curriculum can be adapted for grades 4-8. For a complete list of publications write to:

Food First
Institute for Food and Development Policy
1885 Mission Street
San Francisco, CA 94103

4.
Make Your Own Convenience Foods

Homemade "Hamburger Helper"*

You can make your own convenience noodle and seasoning mix for about one third of the cost of a package of supermarket Hamburger Helper. Children will enjoy helping with this project.

Set out as many plastic bags as the number you wish to prepare of these make-ahead packages. Into each bag place one set of the ingredients listed.

*Adapted and reprinted with permission from Macmillan Publishing Company from *Make Your Own Convenience Foods* by Don and Joan German. Copyright © 1979 by Book Creations.

Italian-Style

In each plastic bag mix together:

8 ounces uncooked broad noodles	½ teaspoon garlic powder
1 tablespoon dried onion flakes	½ teaspoon basil
¼ teaspoon oregano	¼ - ½ teaspoon salt

To cook, lightly brown in a large skillet:
    ¾ lb. ground beef

Add:
    3 ½ cups water and bring to boil. Then add:
    1 package of mix
    1 8-ounce can tomato sauce

Let simmer, stirring often for about 20 minutes, or until noodles are done to taste. Serve with parmesan cheese if desired. Serves 4.

Stroganoff-Style

Mix together in each bag:

8 ounces noodles	1 cup instant nonfat dry milk
1 tablespoon dried onion flakes	½ teaspoon paprika
¾ teaspoon salt	⅛ teaspoon black pepper

To cook, lightly brown ¾ lb. ground beef with 1 cup sliced mushrooms. Then add 4 cups water and 1 tablespoon vinegar. Bring to boil, then add 1 package of mix. Simmer, stirring often about 20 minutes.

Tuna and Noodles
Mix together in each bag:

8 ounces noodles	2 teaspoons dried celery leaves
1 cup instant dry milk	½ teaspoon dry mustard
1 tablespoon flour	¾ teaspoon salt
1 teaspoon paprika	⅛ teaspoon black pepper

To cook, bring to boil 4 cups of water. Add 1 package of mix. Let simmer 15 minutes. Then add one 6½-ounce can of tuna. (If you use water packed tuna add a pat of butter). Let simmer for 5 more minutes.

You can create additional variations. Sausage or tuna could be used in place of beef in the Italian-style. Leftover cooked chicken or pork could be used instead of tuna in the tuna and noodle recipe. A cup of grated Cheddar cheese could be added to the tuna and noodle recipe at the end of the simmering period.

Seasoned Rice Mixes*

No need to pay inflated prices for seasoned rice mixes in the supermarket when it is so simple to make your own.

Seasoned Rice for Chicken

To one cup of brown rice add ½ teaspoon each of the following: garlic powder, thyme, sage, dried celery leaves, ¼ teaspoon of salt, and ⅛ teaspoon of black pepper.

Cook according to your favorite method for cooking rice.

---

*Adapted and reprinted with permission from Macmillan Publishing Company from *Make Your Own Convenience Foods* by Don and Joan German. Copyright © 1979

Seasoned Rice for Beef

To one cup of brown rice add ½ teaspoon marjoram, ¼ teaspoon garlic powder, 1½ teaspoons dried onion flakes, ¼ teaspoon salt, and ⅛ teaspoon black pepper. For extra flavor omit salt and use 1 teaspoon Tamari (soy) sauce when cooking the rice.

● ● ● ● ●

Fabulous Frittatas

"Frittata" (Italian for omlet) is a quickly prepared, satisfying main dish for supper or for a hearty breakfast. Since a frittata is just as good cold as hot you can pack a slice in your brown bag lunch.

Carrot Frittata

1 cup shredded carrots	½ teaspoon celery salt
½ cup chopped onion	¼ teaspoon thyme or
½ cup water	marjoram (optional)
8 eggs	⅛ teaspoon pepper
½ cup milk	carrot slices, parsley sprigs
½ teaspoon dry mustard	for garnish

Combine carrot, onion, and water in 10-inch skillet with ovenproof handle. Cover and cook over medium-high heat until carrots are tender (about 5 minutes). Beat together eggs, milk, and seasonings. Stir in carrot-onion mixture. Melt butter in same skillet. Pour egg-carrot mixture into skillet. Cook over low to medium heat until eggs are almost set, 9 to 10 minutes. Broil about 6 inches from heat until eggs are completely set (about 3-4 minutes). Garnish with parsley and slices of carrots if desired. Cut into wedges and serve from pan. Serve with grated Parmesan cheese if desired. Serves four generously.

Macaroni and Cheese Frittata

2 tablespoons butter	1 cup cooked elbow macaroni
8 eggs	(about ½ cup uncooked)
½ cup milk	1 cup shredded Cheddar cheese
⅛ teaspoon pepper	parsley sprigs, tomato wedges to garnish (optional)

Beat eggs and add remaining ingredients. Follow cooking method for Carrot Frittata above. Serves four generously.

You can create your own frittata variations using different vegetables, such as corn, mushrooms, broccoli, or spinach combined with your favorite herbs for seasoning.

● ● ● ● ●

Quick Ways with Potatoes

The potato, one of America's favorite foods, is a nutrient-dense food. It delivers a high amount of important nutrients in proportion to its calorie count. Easy-to-prepare potato main dishes do not have to come out of boxes. Make a collection of recipes and ideas for quick and easy ways of cooking with unprocessed potatoes. Here are a few to start with.

Oven "French Fries"

For each person to be served, scrub one large potato. Cut unpeeled potato into french fry size strips. In a bowl pour about 1 tablespoon vegetable oil per potato. Toss potato strips in oil, coating them lightly. Spread strips on ungreased baking sheet. Bake at 425° for 10 minutes and then at 350° until done (about 15-20 minutes). Turn with spatula at least once during baking. Season lightly with salt or for variety use a mix of garlic and onion powder.

Oven Parmesan Chips

For each person to be served, scrub one large potato. Cut unpeeled potato in ⅛ inch slices. Place in single layer on lightly oiled baking sheets. For each potato used, melt 1 tablespoon of butter with ⅛ teaspoon of onion powder and a dash of paprika. Brush butter mixture on potatoes and bake for 15 minutes at 400°, or until potatoes are crisp and golden. Sprinkle with Parmesan cheese and serve at once.

Oven-Baked Herbed Potatoes. Herbs impart a marvelous flavor during baking!

4 large potatoes	1 teaspoon dried leaf thyme, crumbled
3 tablespoons butter	
1 tablespoon vinegar	1 teaspoon oregano
½ teaspoon garlic powder	

Scrub potatoes. Cut unpeeled potatoes into ¼ inch thick lengthwise strips. In small bowl combine remaining ingredients and brush this on both sides of the potato slices. Place on lightly greased baking sheet and bake at 400° for 10 minutes. Turn and bake 10 minutes longer or until potatoes are tender.

Lemony-Dill Potato Slices

4 large potatoes	¼ teaspoon salt
3 tablespoons butter	1 ½ teaspoons dried dill weed
1 tablespoon lemon juice	¼ teaspoon pepper

Follow the method for preparing Oven-Baked Herbed Potatoes given on page 56.

Convenience Dishes from Potatoes Cooked in Their Skins
Scrub enough medium-sized potatoes to fill your largest cooking pot. Cook until tender—no longer. Drain. Serve hot, freshly cooked potatoes with generous amounts of cottage cheese which has been seasoned with chives or dried dill weed. Other tasty toppings are: creamed spinach with chopped hard-cooked eggs, creamed peas, or broccoli bits in cheese sauce.

The leftover cooked potatoes, stored in refrigerator, are ready to use in the following recipes.

Potatoes O'Brien

5 medium cooked potatoes	2 tablespoons of oil
2 medium onions, chopped	⅛ teaspoon paprika
1 small green pepper chopped	⅛ teaspoon pepper

Cut potatoes into 1 inch cubes. In a large skillet, cook onions and green peppers in oil until tender. Add potatoes and sprinkle with pepper and paprika. Cook over medium heat, turning frequently, until potatoes are browned.

Taco Potatoes

Cut ¼ inch slices of cooked potatoes. Arrange on lightly oiled baking sheet and top with shredded cheese and chopped onion. Dab with chile salsa and place in hot oven until cheese melts and potatoes are thoroughly heated.

Frozen Hash-Brown Potatoes

Coarsely shred cold cooked potatoes. Spread in thin layers on baking sheets and freeze. When thoroughly frozen, remove from baking sheets and store in plastic bags. To use, remove quantity desired from bag and brown lightly in butter.

●●●●●

Alternatives to Ready-to-Eat Cereals

Breakfast Apple-Rice Pudding*

Save some cooked rice from dinner the night before so you can make this breakfast treat quickly. Children will think they're eating dessert!

¼ cup honey or maple syrup	2 cups cooked rice
2 tablespoons butter	2 cups milk
¼ teaspoon cinnamon	½ cup raisins
⅛ teaspoon nutmeg (optional)	¼ cup coconut (optional)
2 apples, chopped	

In saucepan heat first five ingredients until mixture is hot and bubbly. Add cooked rice and milk and raisins. Heat

---

*Reprinted by permission of *Organic Gardening* magazine. Copyright 1984 by Rodale Press, Inc. U.S.A. All rights reserved.

until mixture begins to bubble, but has not reached a full boil. Reduce heat and simmer, stirring occasionally until pudding thickens (about 10 minutes). Sprinkle with coconut and serve.   4-6 servings

Breakfast Oatmeal Pudding

Follow recipe for Breakfast Apple-Rice Pudding, but substitute one cup of quick oats for rice. Cook 5 minutes.

Hearty Breakfast Shake

This is actually cooked cereal that you drink through a straw. Try it with children who haven't learned to like cooked cereal.

1 cup milk	1 tablespoon honey or sugar
½ very ripe banana	½ cup cooked cereal

Mix milk, banana, and sweetening in blender. Add hot cereal. Blend until smooth. Add more milk if necessary until mixture is thin enough to drink through straw. Makes two small shakes.

Variations:

Use leftover cooked cereal to make a cold shake.

Use fruit juice instead of milk.

Add vanilla to enhance flavor (especially good in cold shake).

Add peanut butter.

Whole Wheat Quick Mix

Pancakes, waffles, muffins, and coffee cake made quickly from this mix are a great substitute for ready-to-eat cereals—less costly and more wholesome.

Measure into large container:
  8 cups whole wheat flour (or part whole wheat and part
    unbleached to total 8 cups)
  3 cups instant dry milk powder
  4 tablespoons plus 2 teaspoons baking powder
  1 teaspoon cream of tartar
  1 teaspoon salt

Mix with pastry blender or wire whip until well blended.
Add 1 ¾ cups of vegetable oil. Mix until well blended. Store
in tightly covered container for one month in refrigerator or
three months in freezer.

Other Breakfast Foods

Pancakes
  2 cups mix
  1 egg
  1 cup water

Mix egg and water together with fork. Add the mix and stir
just to combine. Bake on hot griddle. If you like thicker
pancakes add more mix.
Makes 12 4-inch pancakes.

Waffles
Follow instructions for pancakes except use 2 eggs and
reduce water to ¾ cup.

Coffee Cake
2 cups mix   ¼ cup sugar or honey
1 egg   ½ cup water

Beat egg, sugar, and water together. Add mix, and stir to blend. Spread in oiled 8″ by 8″ cake pan.

Top with:
2 tablespoons softened butter mixed with ½ cup well-diced apples (or other diced fruit, 2 tablespoons honey or sugar, and ½ teaspoon grated orange rind or ½ teaspoon cinnamon.
Bake at 350° for 20 minutes or until it tests done.

Muffins
Follow recipe for coffee cake.
Add one cup blueberries or ½ cup raisins, dried apples, dates, or other dried fruits of your choice. Bake in muffin pan at 375° for 15-20 minutes. Makes 12 medium muffins.

Bake a double recipe of muffins, coffee cake, or waffles. Store in freezer. Remove from freezer the night before you want to serve them for breakfast. In the morning they can be quickly reheated for quick service. Heat waffles in toaster, or under broiler if they are too large to fit in toaster. Muffins and coffee cake can be heated in an electric skillet or large covered pan. Place muffins or coffee cake on a rack in electric skillet, add a little water, cover, and heat until warm and tender. They will taste like they are fresh from your oven!

Make a large batch of French toast. Freeze in single layers on baking sheets. When thoroughly frozen, remove from sheets and store in plastic bag in freezer. To use, remove from bag as many pieces as needed and warm thoroughly in toaster.

Nutrition Tip: Instead of pouring syrup over pancakes, waffles, and French toast, try topping them with applesauce and cinnamon, and a drizzle of syrup if your sweet tooth demands it. A combination of diced apples and banana slices or other fresh fruits in season also makes a tasty, wholesome topping.

● ● ● ● ●

Whipped Topping

When you whip cream, whip double the amount you need. Spoon the extra in serving-size portions on a baking sheet. Freeze, uncovered, then remove from baking sheet and store in plastic bag. (Work quickly to prevent thawing.) Store in freezer up to one month for convenient use the next time you need whipped cream topping.

If you prefer a fat-free whipped topping make *Vanilla Whip.* In small bowl of electric mixer dissolve ½ teaspoon unflavored gelatin in 3 tablespoons of boiling water. Cool to room temperature. Add ⅓ cup ice water and ½ cup instant nonfat dry milk powder. Beat with electric mixer at high speed until peaks form when beater is lifted. Beat in gradually until stiff 2 to 3 tablespoons sugar and ½ teaspoon vanilla. Keeps fluffy up to 2 hours in refrigerator. Stir before serving. Makes 2 cups.

Pudding Mix

Pudding Mix
3 ½ cups instant nonfat   ¾ cup sugar
    dry milk powder   ¾ teaspoon salt
1 cup + 1 tablespoon cornstarch

Combine all ingredients thoroughly. Store tightly covered in cool, dry place.

Vanilla Pudding
Place one cup of mix in saucepan. Gradually stir in 2 cups water. Over medium heat, bring mixture to boil, stirring constantly. Cook gently one minute. Remove from heat. Add ½ teaspoon vanilla and 1-2 teaspoons butter. Pour into serving dishes and refrigerate to set. Makes 4 servings.

Peanut Butter Pudding
Follow directions for Vanilla Pudding, but add ¼ cup peanut butter before cooking. Omit butter.

Chocolate Pudding
Follow directions for vanilla pudding, adding 3 tablespoons cocoa powder to mix before adding water.

Banana Pudding
Pour warm vanilla pudding over sliced bananas. As pudding cools, the banana flavor will permeate the pudding.

Orange Flavored Pudding
For a delicate orange flavor, add ½ teaspoon grated orange rind to warm vanilla pudding.

Notes

Author's Preface

1. John Francis Kavanaugh, *Following Christ in a Consumer Society* (Maryknoll, N.Y.: Orbis Books, 1981).

2. *Food Technology,* May 1984.

3. Ibid.

4. Ibid.

5. "What Is Progress?" *Multinational Monitor,* December 1982, p. 21.

1. Shop for Economy, Nutrition . . . and Justice?

1. Jack Nelson, *Hunger for Justice* (Maryknoll, N.Y.: Orbis Books, 1980), p. 135.

2. "Tax Breaks—Writing Off the Family Farm," *National Impact,* Sept. 1983.

3. Frances Moore Lappe and Joseph Collins, *Food First—Beyond the Myth of Scarcity* (New York: Ballantine Books, 1978).

2. A Supermarket Tour

1. Ibid., p. 283.

2. Ibid., p. 310.

3. Kent Norsworthy, "Top Banana Peels Out of Costa Rica," *Multinational Monitor,* Sept. 1983, p. 5.

4. "Empty Breadbasket? The Coming Challenge to America's Food Supply and What We Can Do About It," *Summary Report of the Cornucopia Project,* Emmaus, Pa., p. 5.

5. "Now, a Diet That Works," *The Cornucopia Project* (Emmaus, Pa.: Rodale Press), p. 10.

6. "What's New in Food Patents," *Food Technology,* May 1984.

7. Ibid.

8. Bonnie Green, "The Canadian Food System: Exposing the Myths," *Coworkers.*

9. Daniel Swerdling, "The Food Monsters," *The Progressive,* March 1980, p. 19.

10. Ibid., p. 19.

11. *Food Technology,* May 1984.

12. Zwerdling, p. 24.

13. "Monopoly on the Cereal Shelves?" *Consumer Reports,* Feb. 1981, p. 17.

14. James B. McGinnis, *Bread and Justice* (Ramsey, N.J.: Paulist Press, 1979), p. 168.

15. Lappe and Collins, p. 330.

3. Work for Change

1. Green.

2. Lappe and Collins, p. 500.

3. *Newsweek,* Feb. 6, 1984, p. 52.

4. *MCC Food and Hunger Notes,* March 1984, p. 11.

Suggested Reading

Byron, William. *The Causes of World Hunger*. Ramsey, N.J.: Paulist Press, 1982. Eighteen causes are discussed in eighteen chapters by prominent scholars such as Arthur Simon, C. D. Freudenberger, Jayne Millar-Wood, Mark Hatfield, Myron Augsburger, and Thomas Gumbleton. A valuable resource associated with Bread for the World.

George, Susan and Nigel Paige. *Food for Beginners*. New York: W. W. Norton, 1982. The bleak picture of hunger and poverty is treated in a simple way with a light touch that does not detract from the seriousness of the world problem.

Lappe, Frances Moore, Joseph Collins, David Kinley. *Aid as Obstacle: Twenty Questions About Our Foreign Aid and the Hungry*. San Francisco: Institute for Food and Development Policy, 1980. Results of study of this group when they tackled 20 common problems incurred when food handouts are given. Some steps to take in solving the hunger problem.

——————. *Food First*. Boston: Houghton-Mifflin, 1977 or New York: Ballantine, 1979. Maintains that the earth has ample supplies of food for the total population. Creates hope that hunger-causing structures can be defeated.

Simon, Arthur. *Bread for the World*. Ramsey, N.J.: Paulist Press, 1984. The expanded and updated edition of Simon's award-winning book on hunger and public policy. A basic hunger resource.

McGinnis, James B. *Bread and Justice: Toward a New International Economic Order*. Ramsey, N.J.: Paulist Press, 1979. An explanation of some of the national and international policies that have brought us to our present crisis together with an examination of what the Gospels tell us about justice among people. A companion teacher's guide includes graphs, charts, and other illustrative material.

Nelson, Jack A. *Hunger for Justice: The Politics of Food and Faith.* Maryknoll, N.Y.: Orbis Books, 1980. A thorough analysis of the systematic causes of the world hunger crisis. For the Christian prepared to go beyond concern to understanding and action.

Cookbooks

German, Don and Joan. *Make Your Own Convenience Foods.* New York: Macmillan, 1978. No need to fill your grocery cart with prepackaged highly processed foods. They can easily be made at home for a fraction of the cost.

Leavitt, Sophie. *All New Penny Pincher's Cookbook.* New York: Bantam, 1980. Has a valuable section of "make your own convenience mixes" recipes in addition to other recipes built around smart shopping in the supermarket.

Longacre, Doris Janzen. *More-with-Less Cookbook.* Scottdale, Pa.: Herald Press, 1976. Suggestions on how to eat better and consume less of the world's limited food resources.

The Author

After growing up in Aurora, Ohio, Marilyn Voran attended Goshen College where she majored in home economics. She and her husband, Melvin, now live in Goshen, Indiana, and are the parents of three grown children.

Marilyn's ongoing interest in foods and nutrition has found expression in a variety of work: teaching home economics at Aurora (Ohio) High School and Bethany Christian High School (Goshen), serving as an instructor with the YWCA of Goshen, and providing food service for the Walnut Hill Kindergarten-Day Care Center in Goshen.

A growing concern about the injustice of many people being denied access to an adequate food supply has led to her present work as coordinator for the Food/Hunger/Justice Committee of the Mennonite Central Committee Great Lakes Region. This involves providing resources for helping congregations build awareness of hunger and justice issues—both domestic and worldwide—and suggesting positive steps toward eliminating hunger, by addressing the root causes of hunger problems as well as by providing emergency food aid.

Food and Justice Resources

Cookbooks

More-with-Less Cookbook by Doris Janzen Longacre. A popular cookbook for those who want to eat better but consume less of the world's limited resources. All 500 recipes gathered from Mennonite kitchens have been tested by professional home economists. Recipes from around the world as well as traditional Mennonite favorites. Spiral-bound for easy use. 328 pages.

Loaves and Fishes by Linda Hunt, Marianne Frase, and Doris Liebert. A children's cookbook that introduces healthy eating in a world of limited resources. 176 pages.

Other Books

Living More with Less by Doris Janzen Longacre. A pattern for living with less and a wealth of practical suggestions from the worldwide experiences of Mennonites. 304 pages.

Living More with Less Study Action Guide by Delores Histand Friesen. Contains projects, questions, and resources for each of the fifteen chapters of *Living More with Less* (above). 112 pages.

Experiencing More with Less by Meredith Sommers Dregni. A five-session intergenerational curriculum for camps, retreats, and other educational settings. 104 pages.

Fund-Raising Projects with a World Hunger Emphasis by Paul Longacre. Twenty-one ideas for families or groups to use for supporting food development programs around the world. 72 pages.

Hunger Awareness Dinners by Aileen Van Beilen. A planning manual for three meals to help persons participate symbolically in world food inequities. 48 pages.

The books above are available at your local bookstore or from HERALD PRESS, Scottdale, Pa. 15683, or Kitchener, Ont. N2G 4M5.